come down the stairs

poems by

Harriet Gleeson

Finishing Line Press
Georgetown, Kentucky

come down the stairs

ACKNOWLEDGMENTS

A version of "desire" appeared in *Mendocino Arts*.

Thanks to Nancy Chinn for her loving support and unfailing belief in this
project. Thanks also to the members of my writing group for support and
critical input.

Publisher: Leah Maines

Editor: Christen Kincaid

Cover Art: Harriet Gleeson

Author Photo: Richard Hubacek

Cover Design: Elizabeth Maines McCleavy

Printed in the USA on acid-free paper.
Order online: www.finishinglinepress.com
          also available on amazon.com

Author inquiries and mail orders:
Finishing Line Press
P. O. Box 1626
Georgetown, Kentucky 40324
U. S. A.

Table of Contents

come down the stairs 1

the little plane that did.. 2

he wanted more 3

faith and flesh 4

how we are made 5

arrivals and departures 7

life's anxieties start early 8

to each her own cage... 9

kid math... 10

making home 12

outfitted for life 13

no such thing as a blank page 14

how waiting goes 15

when the landscape gets weird 16

dia de los muertos 17

rehearsal for the big one 18

freefall 19

desire 22

three score and ten 23

music of a life 25

always a turning... 26

eclipse... 27

meddling with the universe 28

come down the stairs

into the cool
sun's blare muffled
light filtered through slats

this space
below the space
where people
live is tall
the house on stilts

under the house
a place
for a child
to gather
weeds
gray sand
shards of mirror
fabricate magic gardens

a place to watch
while ant lions lie in wait

the little plane that did

the smell of bananas
conjures a wooden lunch box
stained and polished
made for the five-year-old
by her dad

a metal catch small fingers
could unlatch
handle to swing it
on the way to school

Little Pedro
cut from plywood
painted
fastened
to the top

(Little Pedro fat little airplane
flew alone
across the Andes
through thunderstorms)

he wanted more

her father
whistled at twilight
as water fell
from the lightly held hose
sang as he stroked strawberries
from their plants
eased sweet lettuce from the ground

led family holiday singing lustily
the last note of *Daisy, Daisy,*
give me your answer do…
bicycle built for two
ritually morphing into
 little girls in blue

he exploded in energetic bursts of
Figaro in the kitchen
with simple faith
sang the old sacred songs
that loaned themselves
to enthusiastic
and emotional participation
Faith of our fathers living still
in spite of dungeon, fire and sword...
we will be true to thee till death

as a young man
he had yearned to loose his voice
on a wider stage
but a jealous sister-in-law manipulated
an end to his singing lessons

nevertheless
all this he sang
in velvet timbre baritone

faith and flesh

it was something we did
at Blessed Oliver Plunkett Catholic church
three o'clock every Sunday afternoon
in the nineteen forties

gold embroidery gleamed
draped hands grasped the stem
of the golden sunburst
swept cruciform blessing
over heads bowed
before the consecrated host

divinity hidden in a small white disk
all the players in this small drama
of form and persona
life's camouflage
many layers as painfully peeled
as Clarence's dragon skin

altar boys in lace surplices swung censers
twitched ritual clashes with chain and vessel
bells tinkled small children scrambled up and
down from their knees
shuffled under Sister's eye
as Father Cain enveloped in gold on gold
turned a twenty minute ritual into a major performance
involving three stage-right entrances

we sang O Salutaris Hostia
and our eyes followed curls of incense
filtering to heaven perhaps

how we are made

I
the child squinted in bright light
kneaded her bare feet through thick lawn
climbed the fence
teetered arms held out
a trapeze star

clambered to the womb of the mango tree
cool
secret
safe to dare
be the heroes of her books

brave the ocean in sail and steam
prowl a moonlit sky for enemy marauders
run with Flicka and
String Lug the Fox

II
she soared in a world
a book away
crashed as her mother's
erratic screams erupted once
again

footsteps and fury
sounded back
and forth
back and
forth

back

forth

III
meanwhile
her father
gentle man
had left the house

arrivals and departures

butcher birds perch on the Queenslander roof
flute early morning songs
to get the free food flowing

first in the pecking order is Toby
the magpie patriarch
who with his chicks commands the grass

this day Toby chases his chicks from the handouts
it is time for them to move
on find their own territory
make way for the new brood

my Dad is having trouble letting the magpie juveniles go
like last year and the years before that
he staggers across the grass on aching bandy legs
wields a milk bottle like a club
sounds imprecations at Toby

well used to the annual ritual
Toby not impressed lurches away
over the lawn
casts glances over his shoulder
gauging to a nicety when he can stop

but nature wins the bottle battle
and the young birds move on

next year Toby returns with his new brood
to find the universe awry
the man
the food
the bottle
all gone

life's anxieties start early

the child crept down her aunt's stairs
heard that cousin
seated on the sand under the house
playing at the truck driver he became

wheel on rebar for steering
wooden gear stick rooted in the ground
he stamped his feet in the dirt
to slam his gear changes home
roared revving noises
wrenched the wheels of his truck
round imagined highway curves

she escaped
without being noticed

to each her own cage

heartbeats thud
against imprisoning
fingers
neck strains
tiny body
spasms
towards
freedom

the man who holds the bird
gentles fear away
this sorcerer can charm
a bird to trust

except his mate

that frantic creature
will not be calmed
the healing presence she
does not understand
drives her to fury

she shreds her wings
on the bars
she forges
every day

kid math

when I was five or six
pick up sticks
a friend of my fathers returned from the war
to his daughter
his wife going or gone to someone else

did she say anything?
I'm leaving and she's yours
I don't want her?

hard to imagine
but it happens
another mother
called to the school
defiant daughter by her side
looked at her daughter
looked in my eyes
and grated
of course I don't love her

so I know it happens
the dad and his daughter came
to stay at our house
slept on our front verandah

one-two buckle my shoe
three-four knock at the door
we skipped rope
hop-scotched

on the day they moved out
I gave her my doll
whose head could be twisted
and babycurved arms and legs
held by thread through shoulders and hips
could be moved up and down

five six
pick up sticks

making home

some creatures carry their house on their back; it seems like
home is anywhere along the track. it seems like

after years of storms and stress
the roof can easily develop a crack. it seems like

the waters that wash the windows
turn to brack. it seems like

eventually the whole structure
falls into wrack. it seems like

until the heart work is done
we can't get our home back.

it seems like.

outfitted for life

a morning spent
removing and replacing
garments from the closet
what goes with which
drat that spot
should've washed this shirt
long time ago
outfits to wear to my love's 50th college reunion
love is patient
love is kind
love demands
the day was redeemed in the p.m.
at the community fire drill prizes were drawn
I won
a bright red
shiny new
emergency road backpack with
thirteen function
pocket knife
whistle with compass and mirror
jumper cables and and …
you can imagine the rest

no such thing as a blank page

silken under my palm
unspoiled white pages
smell of fresh starts and possibilities

I sweep my hand across the sheet
scratch skin on torn remnants of
pages I have tried to remove
but
they re-appear willy-nilly
Pandora's papers
written in indelible ink

no time now for new stories
plot lines are exhausted
inactive verbs
unnecessary articles
misplaced participles
they're there they're done
the pen having writ
moved moves on

so now   what to do?

if I hurry there is perhaps time
to craft closing chapters
gather loose threads of things done
and things not done
get the protagonists and antagonists into
the same room
find the resolution absolution
craft the dialogue
that asks forgiveness and forgives

how waiting goes

I wait for the results
of a thyroid biopsy while

on every TV channel Roger Ebert
half his face carved away speaks
with his computer voice

my love gasps *it terrifies me*

I whisper *see how alive he looks*

she gags *it's thyroid cancer*

see see how alive
his eyes look I breathe

when the landscape gets weird

the young nun feels like a hole in the landscape
of bright colors flowing
around her on the humid city street.
black robes   veil   sleeves   gloves,
some say her kind are crows—or penguins
a black hole...?...into which everything is
absorbed, everything disappears....
a wormhole, conduit to other realities...?

a pride of young Goths emerges from its own wormhole
on the footpath ahead of her
muscles its way forward.
a female in the pack
makes eye contact.
her conspirator's grin outlined in cadmium red
seduces a smile
there are two of us, the grin says
who do not fit.

dia de los muertos

trees emerge and dissolve in dense fog

as I tramp the pygmy forest
old photos I've been handling float
through my mind
Kate & Patrick John & Harriet Steve & Ettie
their faded faces
set by digital technology to live
beyond these traces
beyond the reflections in this childless only child

my boot strikes a stone
and it rolls for too long
I resist turning to see which ghost
follows me
and walk on to encounter a pile
of deep purple bear scat centered
on its lavender colored
huckleberry season
doily

rehearsal for the big one

the plane climbs to cruising height
passengers scan magazines, gaze out windows

between one breath
and another

the floor
the seat
everything
shudders

metallic noises
clatter bizarre requiem

I make no sound
my feet press into the floor
as if the floor itself
will not fall
through headphones tuned to channel 9
I hear the pilot tell the tower
an engine is not functioning
that he cannot stay up to dump fuel
that there are two hundred forty-seven
souls on board

I feel the careful silence of those
two hundred forty-seven souls
watch the flight attendant huddle over the phone

touch the hand of the one I love

pray

freefall

Annie Leibovitz and David Parsons
Photo shoot, Chrysler Building, NY. 1991

imagine
you stand
feet
astride
a hollow
on a
gargoyle
jutting
from the
61st
floor
on a
surface
not much
wider
than
your
body
camera
in hand
shoot
shout
encouragement

imagine
you drape
like a
sphinx
naked
or stand
on
one foot
arms
raised back arched
on a
gargoyle
jutting
from the
61st
floor
on a
surface
not much
wider
than
your
body

imagine
if death
comes
flings
you
into
irresistible
flight
do you
think the
dare
worthwhile
glide
open-
armed
mouthing
exultation
to the
rushing
air

or

just

fall

desire

points of light litter the night sky
enter the heart like barbs at the end of
lines tugging up up and away

the dog has not noticed the stars
I look down to see her
nose pulsing
examining one side of a grass stem
then the other so delicately
the blade does not stir
intimate with the things of earth

and desire to know the earth so closely
inserts its hooks
and here I am
suspended between desires

three score and ten

I
so far so good
though I've had a scare or two

I've been through the forgetting-words syndrome
four or five times can't remember exactly
words take to hiding just out of reach
like some smug cat
sitting tail neatly furled
ignoring all crooned invitations

so I work to be calm
to let go
it will come

won't it?

II
my dog is a little grey around the muzzle
she runs alerts chases loves amuses
no fear about what might happen
no regrets
just does what she can must do
one day she'll run out of energy
and lie down to die
no fuss

I on the other hand   wonder
when how   wonder
what next   wonder
what this life-task is all about

III
nodules of orange soil
crunch under my feet
I clamber over gullies carved by winter rain
pygmy pines manzanita huckleberry
huddle in the fragile landscape
the dog leaps wild after scent runs
figures of eight corners
in billowing dust flies
over clumps of scrub

from a distance I hear breathy yelps
she can't keep up with life's possibilities.

music of a life
dom gabriel O.S.B

My life is like this Kyrie
the old monk said

and sang

his hand drew the chant
on an old school blackboard
chalk tracing an unbroken line
forward back
gracious curves and sharp reverses
as his voice swelled and ebbed with the melody

God my lover never let me go
through joy, regret or sorrow

then the chalk line meandered to horizontal
life's melody—sung sketched and lived—
almost resolved

I waited in faith, hope and love
for love of all things

the life I lived I lived in Christ
the death I die I die in Christ

always a turning

embers glow
in the branches of maples
spun ropes and nets glitter
on piñon and manzanita

geese screech south
head to tail
strung across a fourth of the sky
reshape to bow vee   bow

light shafts
from meadows of ice flowers
each blossom a cluster
of crystal buddha fingers

scarlet and pink buds
appear where berries have not long gone
the center of roads burn
with fallen redwood feathers

the seasons the years
pulled by grey whale
pursued by orca

death and life
partners on the dancefloor of being

eclipse

we lounge under the apricot tree
waiting while the cosmos arranges
dance of sun and moon

as the surroundings darken
Mary speaks
slowly
as Mary has always done
I came to tell you I'm sliding into Alzheimer's
I'm not writing
can't use my computer any more
I got lost coming here this time

the moon glides across the face of the sun
bends languid light between
wind-blown leaves of the apricot tree
making clusters of crescent shadows dance on the wall

we use our cameras
to freeze the fantastical minuet in digital memory

meddling with the universe

I place an urn and a metal
mandala in (if I say so myself)
harmonious relationship with a slender tree trunk

place a curve of rocks

place a complimentary curve

nearby a retired
wheelbarrow rusts
a crop of strawberries
into existence

Harriet Gleeson was born, an only child, in Queensland, Australia. She grew up with humid weather, mango trees and her Irish Granny next door. She attended twelve years of Catholic school in the days when the protestant kids chanted 'Catholic dogs jump like frogs into the holy water'. She was a pious child, attempting, but I believe never completing, the nine First Fridays (a missed chance to amass celestial brownie points for shorter time in Purgatory.)

She lived as a religious sister for thirty years, graduated from the University of New South Wales in science and math and taught in the order's schools. Notwithstanding the math/science, she has loved literature, especially poetry, all her life.

She moved to the US in 1993 and retired with her partner to California's north coast in 2001 where she discovered a community rich in the practice of the arts, including a lively writing community. The popular community writing classes and their gifted teachers nurtured her unexplored itch to write. She scratched it grandly and with some trepidation by beginning to write poetry.

This long-awaited book is the first fruits of her efforts.

www.ingramcontent.com/pod-product-compliance
Lightning Source LLC
LaVergne TN
LVHW050046090426
835510LV00043B/3327